Hansel and Gretel

AF584079

George Ivanoff

Illustrated by Diane Le Feyer

Once upon a time,
there was a story about two children.
The children ate part of a
gingerbread house.

Sarah and Joe went to the library
to read the story.
As they started to read...

...a fairy appeared!
"I am Fifi the Fairytale Fixit Fairy," she said.
"This story is broken.
Can you help me fix it?"

Fifi waved her wand.

Sarah and Joe fell into the book.

They landed beside a house
made of gingerbread.

A grumpy witch stood by the door.
“What’s wrong?” asked Sarah.

“Those children will not eat my house,” complained the witch.

"You have to eat the house," said Sarah to the children. "Or there won't be a story."

The children shook their heads.
"We don't like gingerbread," they said.

“What do you like?” asked Joe.
“Vegetables,” said Gretel.
“We really like turnips,” said Hansel.

“Can you make your house out of turnips?” Sarah asked the witch.

“I’m not baking a new house,” grumbled the witch.

"You can do magic," said Joe.
"Can you make the house taste like turnips?"
"I could do that," said the witch.

The witch cast a spell.
It made the house taste like turnips.

"Thank you for fixing the story," said Fifi.
"Would you like to eat some of the house?"
"Yuck!" said Joe.
"We don't like turnips!" said Sarah.